Counting
Wipe-Clean Activity Book

for ages 3-5

This CGP wipe-clean book is full of colourful counting activities for Pre-School and Reception children.

It's a fun way to introduce the essential skills — and you can wipe it clean to enjoy again and again!

Helpful Hints

- Use the pen provided to write or draw your answers. You can practise the numbers as many times as you want to. Just wipe the pen away once you have finished the page and have another go.

- Keep the pen away from your eyes. Avoid getting the ink on clothing, furniture or fabric as it may not be washable.

- A grown-up can help you read the questions. Let them know which activities you enjoy the most.

- Find a nice place to work. Make sure you're comfortable at your desk or table.

- Writing the numbers nice and clearly is really important. Work neatly, and try to keep your pen inside the lines.

- 'Cafe Chaos!' in the centre covers the numbers 0-20 — you may want to save this until last.

Published by CGP
ISBN: 978 1 78908 970 7

Editors: Keith Blackhall, Hannah Lawson,
Duncan Lindsay, Gabrielle Richardson, Rachael Rogers

With thanks to Catherine Heygate and
Gareth Mitchell for the proofreading.
With thanks to Alice Dent for the copyright research.

Printed by Elanders Ltd, Newcastle upon Tyne.

Cover and graphics used throughout the book © Educlips
Cover design concept by emc design ltd.

Text, design, layout and original illustrations
© Coordination Group Publications Ltd. (CGP) 2023
All rights reserved.

CGP, Broughton House, Griffin Street,
Broughton-in-Furness, Cumbria, LA20 6HH

CGP c/o Elanders GmbH, Anton-Schmidt-Str. 15,
71332 Waiblingen, GERMANY

Photocopying this book is not permitted, even if you have a CLA licence.
Extra copies are available from CGP with next day delivery • 0800 1712 712 • www.cgpbooks.co.uk

Contents

The Numbers 1 to 4	2
The Numbers 5 to 7	4
The Numbers 8 to 10	6
Counting up to 10	8
Cafe Chaos!	10
More or Less	12
Finding the Same	14
The Numbers 11 to 15	16
The Numbers 16 to 20	18
Counting up to 20	20
Counting Crates	22

The Numbers 1 to 4

First Try This

Count the number of things in each group.
Then, trace the numbers.

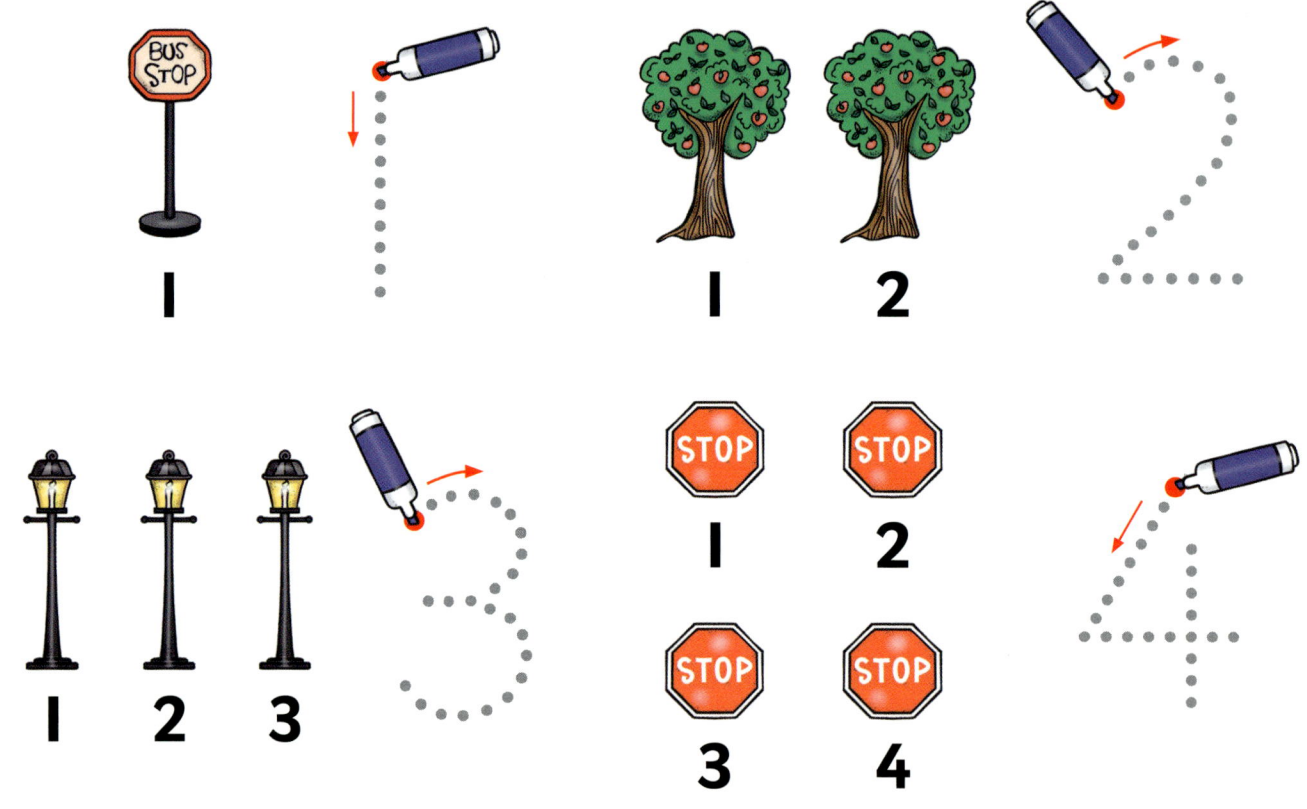

Now Try These

Count the wheels in each picture.
Draw lines to match the pictures to the correct numbers.

1   2

Circle the plate with 2 pieces of gingerbread on it.

Count the pencils on the desk.
Trace the correct number.

 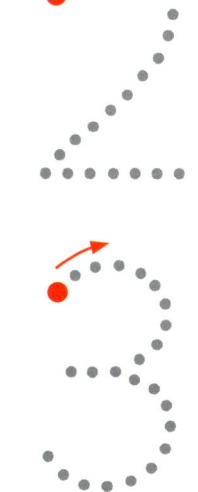

Draw 4 balls in the goal.

Well done you! You can count from 1 to 4. Draw a smiley face.

The Numbers 5 to 7

First Try This

Count the number of things in each group.
Then, trace the numbers.

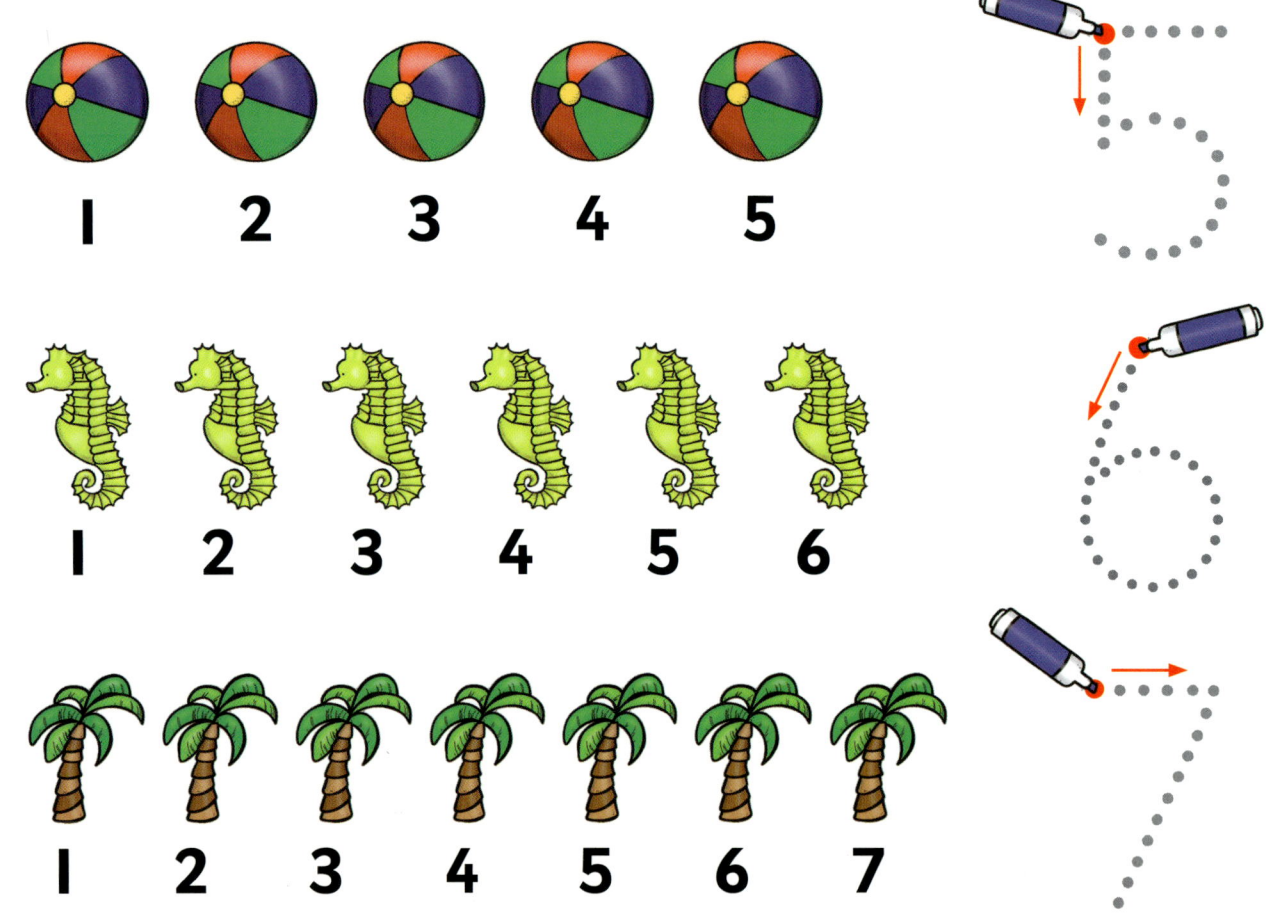

Now Try These

Count the shrimps in each rock pool.
Circle the rock pool with 5 shrimps in.

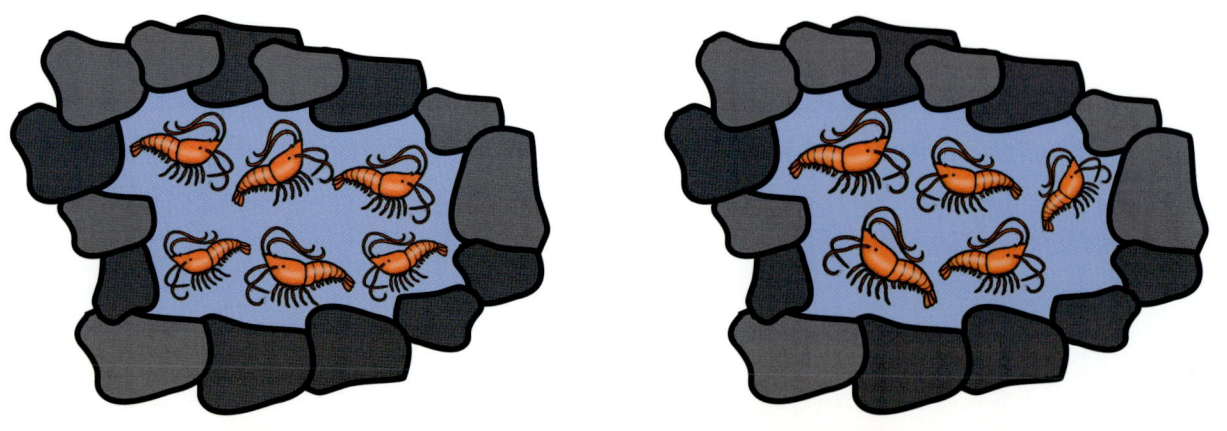

Draw more fish so there are 6 fish in the tank.

Count the buckets. Write how many there are in the box.

Draw 5 flags (🚩) on the sandcastle. Then, circle 7 starfish.

Counting from 5 to 7 is no problem for you! Draw a smiley face.

The Numbers 8 to 10

First Try This

Count the number of things in each group.
Then, trace the numbers.

1 2 3 4 5 6 7 8

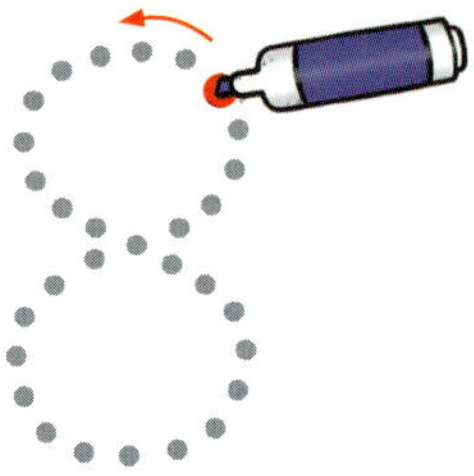

1 2 3 4 5 6 7 8 9

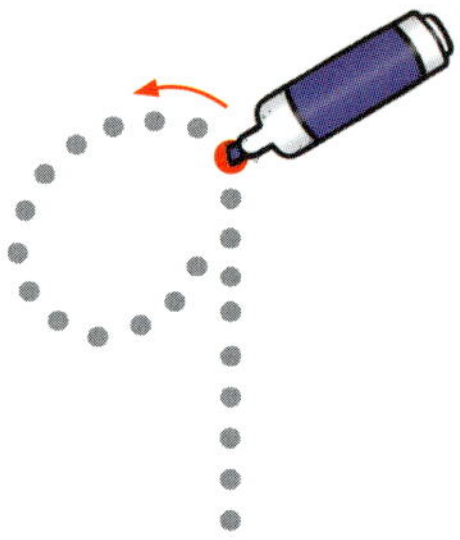

1 2 3 4 5 6 7 8 9 10

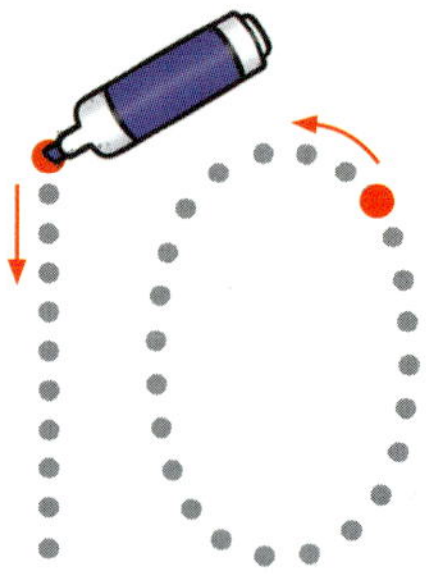

Now Try These

Draw 9 eggs (🥚) in the space below.
Then, write the number 9 next to the eggs.

Count the hay bales () in each pile. Circle the pile with 10 in it.

Count the tractors. Write how many there are in the box.

Count the animals in each group. Tick the odd one out.

Fantastic! You can count to 8, 9 and 10. Draw a smiley face.

Counting up to 10

First Try This

Count the muffins on each shelf.
Then, draw lines to match each shelf to the correct child.

Now Try These

Count the spots on each bow.   Tick the bow with 3 spots.

 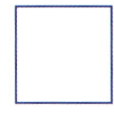    

Count the bees on each hive.   Circle the hive with 4 bees.

Count the shapes in each group. Circle the odd one out.

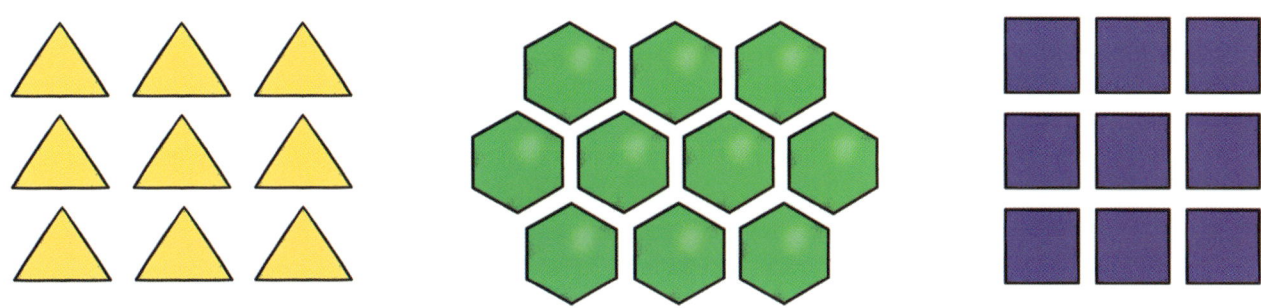

Count how many children there are. Trace the correct number.

Draw 4 more planets (🪐) below. Then, write how many planets there are in total in the box.

Wow! You can count up different things. Draw a smiley face.

 I need 2 **more** ice creams!

Iona

I need 4 **more** donuts!

 Jo

Circle the correct person to answer each question.

Who has more donuts?  Alice    Jo

Who has less ice cream?  Bob    Iona

Who has the same number of items as Bob?  Alice    Hasan

11

More or Less

First Try This

Count the buckets of water that Amy and Billy have. Then, circle the correct words to complete the sentences.

Amy has **more** / **less** water than Billy.

Billy has **more** / **less** water than Amy.

Now Try These

Count the toys on each shelf. Circle the shelf with **more** toys and write the number of toys on that shelf in the box.

Count the cans of food that each dog has.
Tick the box next to the dog who has **less** food.

Count the coins that Ken has.
Draw coins by Jaya so that she has **one more** coin than Ken.

Ken   Jaya

Count the cartons of juice on each table. Write the numbers in the boxes below. Then, circle the table that has **less** juice.

Finding the Same

First Try This

Count the cakes that each child has.
Then, circle the correct names to complete the sentences.

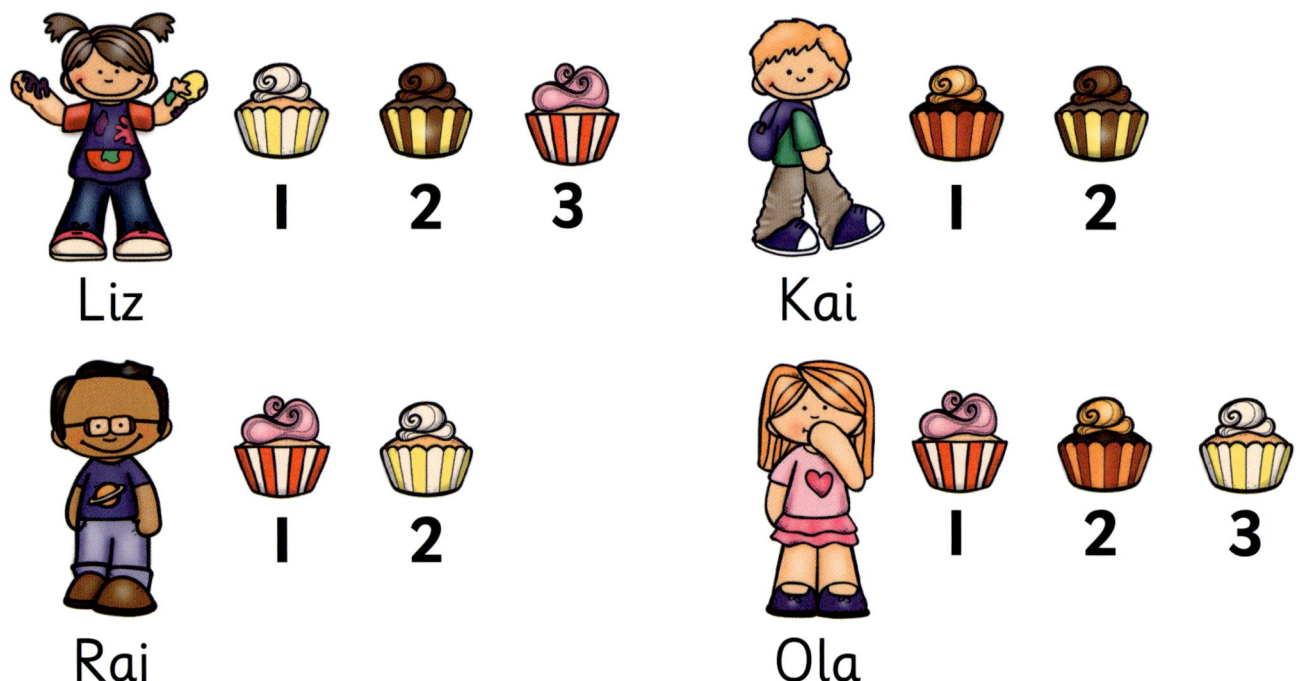

Kai and **Liz** / **Raj** have the same number of cakes.

Ola and **Liz** / **Raj** have the same number of cakes.

Now Try These

Draw lines to match the signs that have the same number of stars.

Count the spiders on the webs. Are there the same number of spiders on each web? Tick your answer.

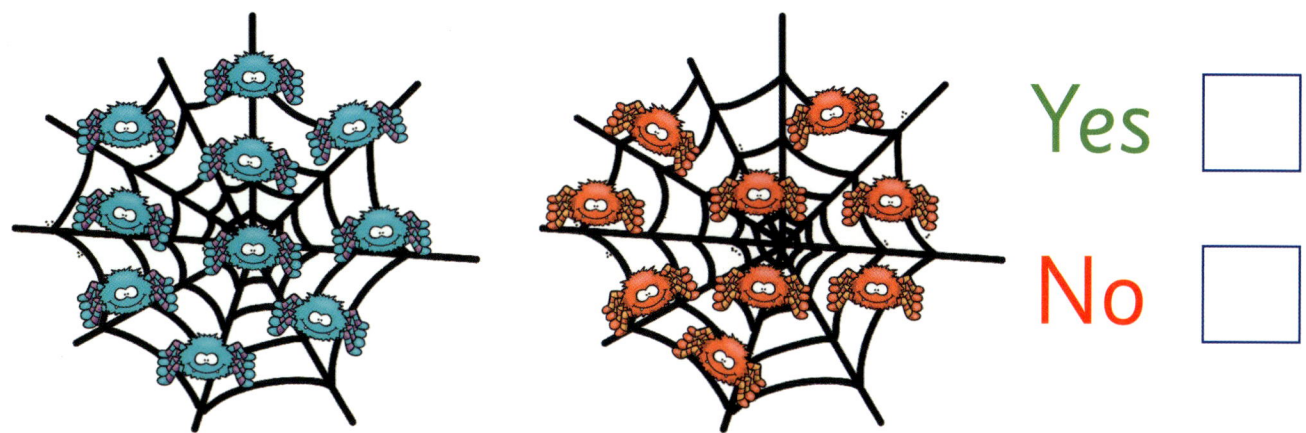

Yes ☐

No ☐

Count the tennis rackets.
Draw some balls so there are the same number of balls and rackets.

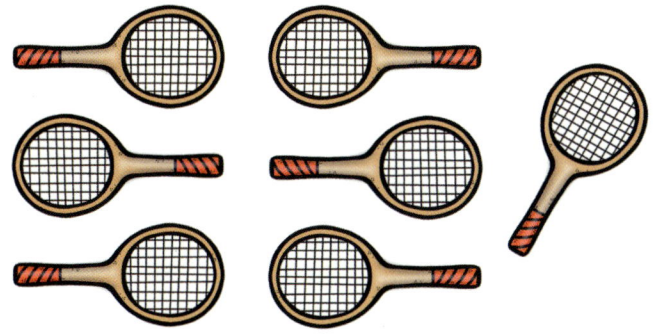

Count the ducks.
Circle the same number of frogs as there are ducks.

Amazing! You can find the same amount. Draw a smiley face.

The Numbers 11 to 15

First Try This

Count the number of things in the group. Then, trace the numbers. As you trace each one, circle the matching number in the group.

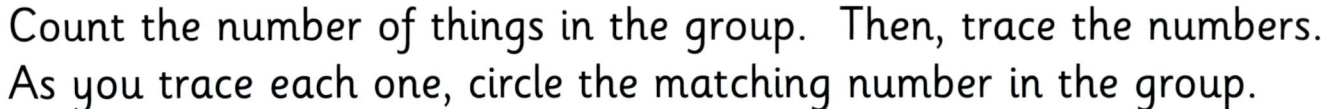

1 2 3 4 5 6 7 8
9 10 11 12 13 14 15

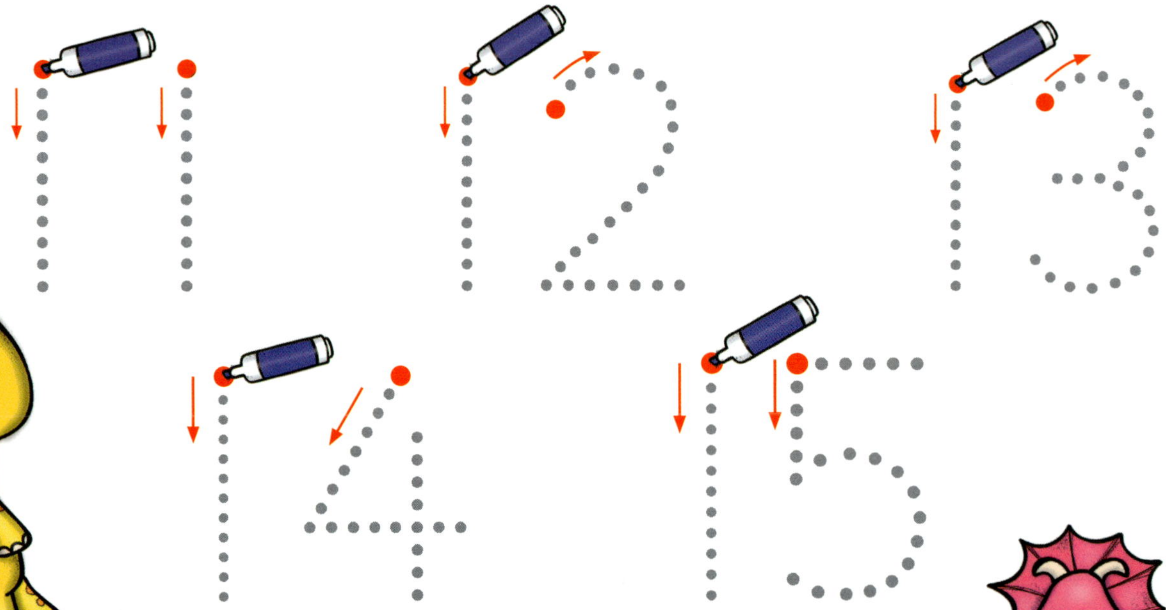

Now Try These

Count the number of shovels. Write the number in the box.

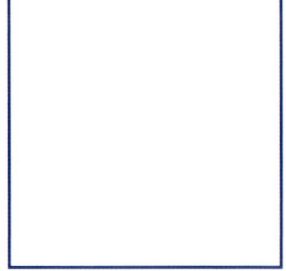

Count the spots on each dinosaur.
Circle the dinosaurs that have 11 spots.

Count the dinosaurs in the nest.
Draw a line to match the nest to the correct number of dinosaurs.

Draw more spikes on the dinosaur's back so that it has 13 in total.

You've mastered counting up to 15! Draw a smiley face.

The Numbers 16 to 20

First Try This

Count the number of things in the group. Then, trace the numbers. As you trace each one, circle the matching number in the group.

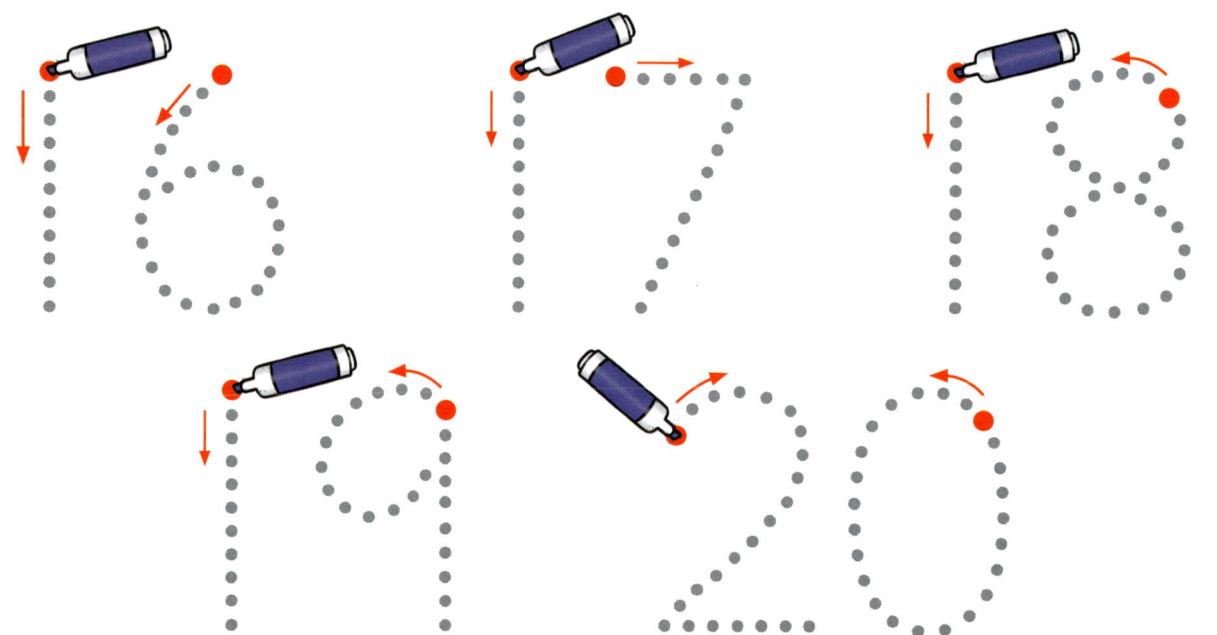

Now Try These

Count the snails. Write how many there are in the box.

Count the vegetables in each box. Draw lines to match each box to the correct number, then trace the numbers.

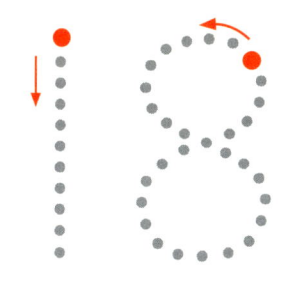

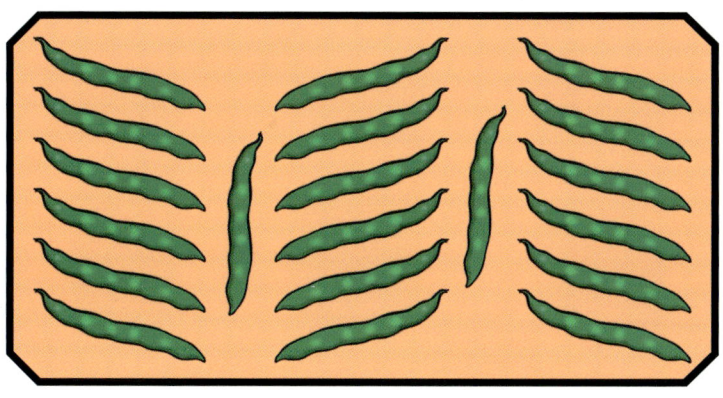

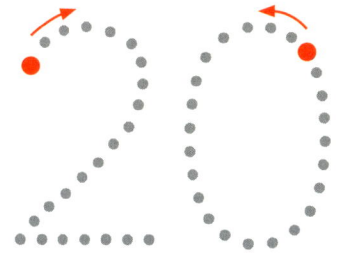

Circle 17 minibeasts.
Then, draw 19 leaves (🍃) in total on the sunflowers.

You've learnt about counting up to 20! Draw a smiley face.

Counting up to 20

First Try This

Count the cacti. Then, trace the number to complete the sentence.

There are 20 cacti.

Now Try These

Circle 15 sunflowers. Then, trace the number 15.

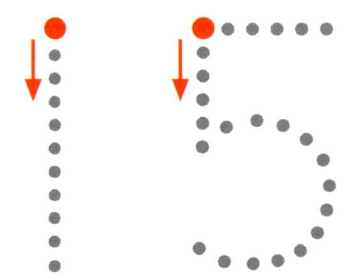

Count the birds in each group. Then, draw lines to match each bird house to the correct group of birds.

How many flowers are there? Write the number in the box.

Draw 11 clouds in the sky.
Give 3 clouds spots and 5 clouds stripes.

Terrific — you can count up to 20! Draw a smiley face.

Counting Crates

Count the objects in each crate.
For each crate, draw the object that there is **more** of in the box.

Count the objects in the crates above to answer the questions.
Write your answers in the boxes.

How many **red** objects are there in total?

How many **blue** objects are there in total?

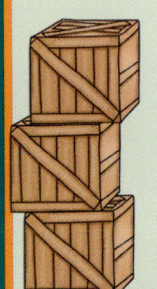